Pete's Street Beat
© 1999 Creative Teaching Press, Inc.
Written by Margaret Allen, Ph.D.
Illustrated by Karl Edwards
Project Director: Luella Connelly
Editor: Joel Kupperstein
Art Director: Tom Cochrane

Published in the United States of America by:
Creative Teaching Press, Inc.
P.O. Box 6017
Cypress, CA 90630-0017

CTP 2913

Street Beat. Street Beat.
What a treat, the Street Beat.

2

Steel drums play.
Stamp your feet.

3

Clap your hands.
Sway to the beat.

4

Street Beat. Street Beat.
Let's meet at Pete's Street Beat.

Rat-a-tat-tat.
Thump-a-thump.

Ring-a-jing-jing.
Bump-a-bump.

Ding-a-ding-dong.
Sing-a-sing-song.

Street Beat sounds all day long.

9

Street Beat. Street Beat.
What a treat, the Street Beat.

10

Meet and eat in the street.

Feel the beat in your feet.

Street Beat. Street Beat.
So, so neat, the Street Beat.

13

Street Beat. Street Beat.
Meet me at Pete's Street Beat.

BOOK 13: Pete's Street Beat

Focus Skills: long e: ee, e-e, ea, ending e

Focus-Skill Words		Sight Word	Story Words
feel	beat	sounds	
feet	eat		
meet	neat		
steel	treat		
street	me		
Pete's			

Focus-Skill Words contain a new skill or sound introduced in this book.

Sight Words are among the most common words encountered in the English language (appearing in this book for the first time in the series).

Story Words appear for the first time in this book and are included to add flavor and interest to the story. They may or may not be decodable.

Interactive Reading Idea

Have your young reader practice long *e* words by working together to make a long-e word collage in the shape of a steel drum. Help your reader draw a drum and cut it out. Look through each line of the story and copy all words that contain the long *e* sound on separate index cards, using a different color marker for each word. Read the words, and then glue them onto the long-e steel-drum collage.